CHUTE!
Air Drop for Defense and Sport

by C. B. COLBY

Coward, McCann & Geoghegan, Inc.   New York

The parachute has graduated from an aviation necessity to a vehicle for sport. Parachute rides are popular at many shore resorts where high-speed boats, with the help of onshore winds, can carry a parachutist aloft on a canopy towed behind a speedboat. The rider starts from shore where the wind preinflates the canopy and is towed at an altitude of a few hundred feet out over the ocean and back for a gentle stand-up landing on the beach. The author took these photos at a Mazatlán, Mexico, resort. Left, a parachutist in harness is about to take off. Right, a chute is towed out over the ocean. The rider wears a life jacket, but dunkings are rare, and rescuers are always at hand.

Contents

Chutes Keep Pace with Air Progress.... 3	Flying Lance and Jeeps...................... 28
"This Is Parachuting?"........................ 6	GPE Saves Time................................ 30
Learning to Land............................... 8	Pull That Clevis Pin............................ 32
Higher and Higher............................ 10	Floating Firebee............................... 34
Student vs. Chute............................. 12	Brake It Gently!................................ 36
The First Real Jump.......................... 14	Funny Car Safety Chute..................... 38
What a Thrill! 16	One Plus Two Equals Safe Stop.......... 39
Back to Back Before Landing.............. 18	U.S. Forest Service Smoke Jumpers.... 40
A HALO for Secrecy.......................... 20	Astronauts Learn How to Dunk........... 42
Heavy Equipment Via Parachute.......... 22	NASA's Parawings and Paragliders.... 44
On Your Mark, Get Set, "Geronimo!" 24	Rehearsal and "For Real"................. 46
Sky-Diving Truck............................... 26	Welcome Sight to Millions................. 48

PHOTO CREDITS

National Aeronautics and Space Administration, pages 37 (bottom), 42, 43, 44, 45, 46, 47, 48, and full-color cover transparency. Teledyne Ryan Aeronautical, pages 34, 35, and title page. Pioneer Parachute Company Inc., and Barish Associates, Inc., pages 5, 37 (top). Leslie Lovett, National Hot Rod Association, pages 38, 39. U.S. Forest Service, U.S. Department of Agriculture, pages 40, 41. U.S. Air Force, pages 6, 12, 13, 14, 15, 17, 36. All others courtesy of the U.S. Army.

Copyright © 1973 by C. B. Colby   All rights reserved.   Printed in the United States of America

Fourth Impression

Library of Congress Catalog Card Number: 73-77424
SBN: GB-698-30447-0
SBN: TR-698-20213-9

Chutes Keep Pace with Air Progress

This revision of my first book about parachutes, *Air Drop*, published in 1953, will show many changes. A great deal has happened in the two decades since *Air Drop* appeared. A good example is the last paragraph of the front copy. There I said, "It's not too wild a guess that parachutes for spaceship landings are being developed in some of our research laboratories and wind tunnels right now." It was true!

Although it is still thrilling, we are now, a few short years later, accustomed to seeing our astronauts come floating down in their command modules under giant orange and white ringsail canopies as they return from the moon and other space missions.

The braking force of the parachute is now being used for other purposes than slowing a man's plunge to earth from a disabled aircraft. It is used to stop aircraft after landing, brake the drag racer to a safe stop, save entire experimental aircraft models, and return satellite packages safely.

Long before anyone had taken to the air in any sort of device, centuries before the Wright brothers made the first powered flight, the safety of all air travelers was assured. As early as 1490 the Italian artist and scientific genius Leonardo da Vinci had made a sketch of a pyramid-shaped parachute and described its use. This sketch is reproduced below.

The da Vinci parachute was never constructed or tested, but in 1607 or 1617 (the date has been long debated) an adventurous Venetian named Fausto Veranzio, is reported to have leaped from a high tower in Venice wearing a somewhat similar "parachute." A sketch of this is also reproduced below. The details of this talented architect's leap have been the subject of much debate.

In spite of Da Vinci's sketch and the various recorded versions of Fausto Veranzio's leap, a French physician by the name of Sébastien Lenormand, is usually officially credited with the invention of the parachute in 1783. His countryman, André Garnerin, is considered the first parachutist. He bailed out over Paris on October 22, 1797, presumably from a disabled balloon.

The parachute has made it possible for man to take to the air in kites, balloons, gliders, airplanes, rockets, and spacecraft, with the assurance that he can return safely to report his sensations and scientific findings. It is impossible to tell just how many lives have been saved by this simple device, but undoubtedly the figure is in the hundreds of thousands. Its importance to aviation and the conquest of space cannot be overestimated. The parachute was first used by balloonists as a last-resort lifesaver. It was also used by recklessly enterprising daredevils who made exhibition parachute jumps from hot-air balloons.

The open parachute was suspended either from the balloon basket or from the bottom opening

The sketch at the left, by Leonardo da Vinci, was included in his manuscript Codex Atlanticus (1490), now in the Ambrosian Library in Milan, Italy. Da Vinci was far ahead of his time with many of his inventions. At the right is a sketch published in *Machinea Novae*, written by the Venetian architect Fausto Veranzio in 1595.

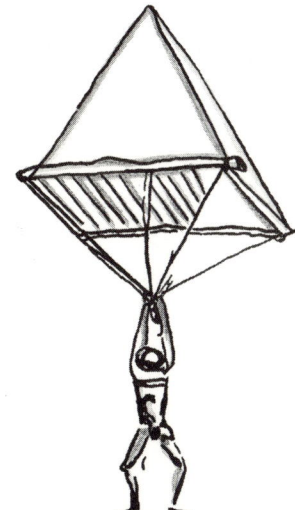

The first parachutes were used in World War I, primarily by airmen in observation balloons. The parachute was hung from the center of its canopy, and the harness was worn by the aviator. In an emergency the aviator merely dived out of the basket, and the chute broke away from the basket. The photo at left shows such a balloon chute being tested. The inverted chutes at left were used to hold the balloon steady. The center photo shows very early parachutes attached to the bottom of an early plane. Ropes ran from the folded chutes to the airmen's harnesses. These chutes were not too reliable. Airmen could only leave the plane when it was in a horizontal position, to be sure of getting good results. The photo at right shows an early type of backpack chute.

of a hot-air balloon. The balloonist wore a harness attached to the shroud lines of the parachute. In an emergency he merely dived over the side of the basket, breaking the chute away from its mooring. The exhibition jumper rode into the air on a trapeze bar below the parachute. When he reached a suitable height, he pulled a cord cutting the parachute free and drifted down.

Jumping out of a drifting balloon was one thing, but leaping from a fast-moving aircraft was quite another. Designers were forced to come up with a brand-new type of canopy—one that could stand up under a great opening shock and that could be folded into a compact unit. A parachute to be used in speedy aircraft had to be securely packaged against high winds, yet be able to open almost instantly, once the airman was free from the aircraft.

During World War I, when aircraft construction was comparatively fragile, with a maze of external wires and struts, parachutes were designed to be attached to the outside of the aircraft in tubes, boxes, or domes. Many proved unsuccessful. Usually a strong rope ran from the packaged chute to a harness worn by the airman; the rope often became entangled in some part of the aircraft, dragging the man to his death still attached to his worthless chute. Also, an airman had to leave the plane on the side on which his static line was attached to the chute package. This was not always possible. Still, the British "Guardian Angel" parachute invented by E. R. Calthrop, packed in a tube attached to the side of the plane fuselage, saved the lives of many lucky British airmen.

This type of chute was later replaced by a similar chute which attached to the bottom of the aircraft. It still required static lines running to a harness, as shown in the photo.

American designers began to experiment with what was called a free-style parachute. This was a parachute worn by the airman himself; no external cord attached the parachute to the aircraft. With such a chute, an airman could easily leave the aircraft during any maneuver from either side, without any danger of becoming entangled in his static line.

The first really successful free-style parachute was designed and demonstrated by Leslie Irvin. Another successful designer of a free-style aerial lifesaver was Floyd Smith. These chutes were worn on the airman's back. All he had to do was leap from the plane, count to ten, and pull a rip cord to open the pack. When he did this, a small, spring loaded pilot chute popped out; this in turn pulled out the main canopy. Over the years the harness, packing, and canopy of the parachute have become stronger, more compact, and more reliable. I have worn various kinds over the years and can vouch for their improved fit and control.

The successful development of the free-style chute was of tremendous importance to both pilot and passenger. Its reliability made mass troop drops a routine military operation. It also brought greater safety to testing of experimental aircraft and to racing, civilian training, search-and-rescue operations, and many otherwise hazardous aerial assignments and operations.

As aircraft speeds increased, new parachutes had to be developed that could withstand still greater opening shocks and provide greater stability, more compact packaging, and more reliable harnesses.

The ejection seat helped solve the escape problem from high-speed aircraft. This combination seat and parachute was literally blown up and out of fighter planes, and bombers, so that the airman was well away from the aircraft before the canopy opened. Even at dangerously low altitudes, the height reached during the ejection permitted many endangered pilots to land safely by parachute.

Ribbon chutes, which used circles of strong ribbon rather than solid canopy, permitted excessive opening pressure to escape between the ribbons instead of splitting the fabric. Various types of splits, extra panels, and vents were also tried.

Special chutes were designed for lowering mines into enemy harbors, for cargoes ranging from small radios to full-sized military trucks and cannon, for frontline troops and for spies behind the lines. Other chutes made possible delivery of mercy supplies to lifeboats, field hospitals, and other disaster victims. Fire fighters dropped into the wilderness used specially designed chutes, while giant ringsail chutes, 80 or 100 feet across, were developed to carry returning spacecraft.

Parachutes were designed for stopping, as well as for dropping. They proved very efficient in stopping high-speed landing aircraft on icy runways in case of brake failure. They were soon used by drag racers to stop their vehicles at the end of a race. Adventurous people began to use parachutes for sky diving, a sport in which the diver bails out from a plane and, instead of opening his parachute, spreads his arms and legs and maneuvers by body movements. The parachute is used in this sport merely for landing.

What the parachute of the future will look like is anyone's guess. Right now we have chutes that come straight down, as well as chutes that can glide for considerable distances under radio control. The chutes of the future will certainly have even more astonishing capabilities.

My sincere appreciation to all who helped with this book, especially "Les" Gaver, chief of the Audio-Visual Division of NASA, Washington, D.C., who helped with the last few pages and the full-color cover.

— C. B. COLBY

It was many years after the first successful parachute was invented that a really new idea came along in parachute design. In 1958 David T. Barish introduced two radically new designs. At the left is one of his vortex ring chutes with four sail-like cloth blades that revolve like a helicopter's rotor blades. These ensure unusual stability and low opening shock. (See also page 37.) Photos at center and right show a three-gore and a five-gore sport parachute also designed by this talented young aeronautical engineering consultant turned inventor. Both are very light in weight (the one at left is only six pounds) and maneuverable.

"This Is Parachuting?"

There is no branch of our armed services that requires better physical conditions than the paratroopers. Particular stress is put upon the back and the muscles of the arms and legs during training and jumping, so special efforts are made to strengthen them during training. Above a pararescueman is doing twenty push-ups while wearing his emergency chest parachute during his training at Fort Benning, Georgia. On the opposite page, students at the 82d Airborne Division's Basic Airborne School at Fort Bragg, North Carolina, do squat-jumps during final physical training tests. These rugged physical tests are given to ensure that the trainees are in good enough condition to undertake the demanding training of the paratroopers. Being in less than top physical condition might endanger not only the jumper but the others who jumped with him. On the following pages you will see why.

Learning to Land

As the old saying goes, "It isn't the coming down that hurts, but the landing that smarts!" The most important part of a paratrooper's training is learning how to land safely with his equipment. Above, in what looks like a paratrooper ballet, four future paratroopers jump from a low training platform into the dirt. Opposite (top) trainees jump from a four-foot platform and roll to absorb the shock as others wait their turn. In the background are two training towers from which trainees will later make their first actual parachute drops. Note the two falling parachutes just behind the instructor in a white T-shirt. The lower photo, opposite, shows trainees learning how to leave a mock aircraft via the door. Each man wears a backpack and an emergency reserve chest pack. The back chute is opened by a static line attached to the rip cord of the chute, so that the parachutist can jump with both hands free. Chest packs are opened by the jumpers themselves in the case of a backpack chute failure. Fortunately this is a rare situation!

Higher and Higher!

As the students progress, they gain enough confidence and skill to undertake more realistic landing simulations. Above, students demonstrate their skill in handling swing landing falls before a visiting general. A landing with a rapidly swinging chute is dangerous and requires special training and skill. Students must know how to handle all types of landings before they actually jump, because the very first landing could be a rough one. On the opposite page, students practice jumps and landings from a 34-foot tower. They exit from a door designed to simulate an aircraft door, and are carried down long cables to the landing area, where they learn to land safely, rolling to prevent injury to themselves and to any equipment they may be carrying. Note the students on lower levels awaiting their turn to make a jump. The motto "Follow me" on the insignia is well chosen.

Student vs. Chute

The student must know how to deflate his canopy once he is safely on the ground, to prevent being dragged across rocks, over a cliff, or into such wartime hazards as a hidden minefield. In order to show a student who has not yet made an actual jump what to expect, his chute is inflated by a powerful wind machine. He is shown how to use the quick release harness to save himself and his equipment from injury. Instructors and other students stand by to help if necessary. On the opposite page is shown an actual landing (top) and (bottom) in which the student pulls the lower shroud lines to spill the wind from the chute. Note the instructor giving instructions through an electric bullhorn while another instructor stands by ready to give a hand if he is needed.

The First Real Jump

A first real parachute jump is made under carefully supervised conditions. It is made from a 250-foot steel tower in the center of a huge dirt drop zone, where instructors can watch every phase of the jump. The canopy of each chute is held open by a steel mesh frame so that it is sure to open when the student is released. Above, a student is fitted into his harness for the ride up. On the opposite page we see this student being lifted by a steel cable for his first ride down beneath his chute. The canopy is held to the rim of the training tower hoop by quick release clips. When the top of the tower is reached, the open canopy is released, and the student is on his way down again. In a very few seconds, he must remember all the landing training and instructions he has received and do everything just right.

What a Thrill!

At the moment of release, a student starts down on his first actual parachute drop. Below, an instructor gives encouragement and instructions through a bullhorn. This is one of the towers at Fort Benning, Georgia. It has four arms shown on the opposite page and can handle three jumpers at a time. The upwind arm is never used so that the student will not be carried into the frame of the tower by the wind. The wind sock on the top of the tower in the opposite photo gives the instructor the wind direction so that he will use the safe three arms. Note that the empty canopy frame has started back down for the next student. It will be ready for use by the time the first jumper has safely landed. Some training centers have more than one of these giant training towers.

Back to Back Before Loading

Once a paratrooper has graduated from his training school and won his silver paratrooper badge he can expect to take part in various exercises in almost any part of the globe. He may see the actual combat service for which he has been trained. Above, a unit of the instant ready forces of the 187th Infantry sit back to back on the airport concrete, waiting for the signal to load. On the opposite page (top) a unit of the 1st Battalion, 509th Airborne Infantry, 8th Infantry Division, prepare to take part in an air drop over Denmark during a joint Danish-American exercise. Below, back in America, personnel of the 101st Airborne Division aboard a C-124 prepare to jump. In both photos you can see the static lines running from the rip cords of the paratroopers' backpacks to the cable along the wall. The hooks and static lines remain attached to the aircraft after the men have jumped. Note the huge packs carried by the troopers in the lower photo. These may weigh as much as eighty-five pounds and contain food, ammunition, weapons, communications equipment, water, clothing, and even demolition equipment. If the pack is extremely heavy, a jumper may have to use his reserve chute to slow his drop. A paratrooper must be ready for anything once on the ground, so he takes supplies and weapons with him.

A HALO for Secrecy

There are several different types of parachute drops. There is the mass tactical jump (opposite), in which a strong force of troops is delivered from several transport planes flying over the drop zone. There is also what is known as the HALO (high altitude low opening) type of delivery. In this type, troopers are dropped at high altitudes; instead of opening their chutes at once, they fall free for several thousand feet and then open their chutes at low altitude. There are several military reasons for the use of the HALO technique, which is basically the same as sky diving for sport. First, it enables the aircraft to fly high enough to escape all but electronic spotting so that the troops can be delivered secretly. Second, it reduces the time the men are coming down under their canopies. Canopies can be spotted in time for the enemy to set up ground defenses against the descending men or even fire upon them as they dangle below their chutes. Falling free for great distances requires special training in body positioning for maneuvering during the fall. Above, a HALO candidate is taught body positions while dangling on the end of a cable in a hangar. The Special Forces Group of the First Army employs HALO troops for special assignments.

Heavy Equipment Via Parachute

There seems to be almost nothing that a parachute cannot handle if the load is well packed and the parachute canopy or canopies are big enough. Here are some of the heavy loads that can be safely dropped by chute, packaged for the drop. Above, a M101A1 105-mm light howitzer rigged for dropping; opposite page, a SPAT (90-mm self-propelled anti-tank vehicle) ready for the plunge (top); and (below) a bulldozer on its base ready for a parachute ride to earth. In all these U.S. Army photos you will notice that there are blocks of material between the equipment and the platform to which it is lashed. This material is designed to crush upon landing impact, absorbing a great deal of the shock of the landing. These units are air-drop-delivered complete with ammunition, fuel, and anything else required to get them into action as soon as they are freed of their platforms, chutes, and lashings. Men are dropped separately, of course, as close as possible to where the equipment will land. Note the winged skull and crossbones insignia on the armor plate of the howitzer above and the giant chutes in packages behind each unit.

On Your Mark, Get Set, "Geronimo!"

The photo above shows a wheeled earth-moving unit on a flatbed trailer ready to be loaded into a cargo plane for air dropping. Note all the crushable blocks packed under and around this heavy unit to help assure a safe landing. On the opposite page is an "Army Mule," a versatile mechanical "mule," packaged for an air drop from the rear door of a C-130 aircaft. A big chute is packaged on top of the vehicle, and a static line extends from the top of the chute to a ring around the heavy steel cable that runs along the wall of the aircraft above the head of the man at left. All the cargo-handling personnel wear parachutes, too, in case they are swept out the door when the vehicle is released. The lower photo shows the vehicle vanishing out the door, leaving the roller cargo panels on the floor of the plane. You can see the static line about to pull out the pilot chute, which in turn will release the huge canopy that lowers the vehicle to the drop zone below. It is quite a sensation to see a piece of heavy equipment leave your aircraft and plunge toward the earth several thousand feet below, even if you are not going with it!

Sky-Diving Truck

This exciting sequence shows the dropping of a two-and-a-half-ton truck from a C-130 Hercules cargo plane, flying at 1,500 feet near Yuma, Arizona. Above, the six giant chutes have just begun to open. The truck, mounted on a base, looks like a box of crackers compared with the chutes; some of these huge cargo chutes measure as much as 80 feet across! On the opposite page (top) we see the six chutes fully inflated and easily lowering the truck. The bottom photo shows the truck just as it touches down without even raising a cloud of dust. The shroud line on the chute at the right is just beginning to go slack. These giant cargo chutes are automatically released after impact. This prevents overturning or dragging of the equipment after the landing. The chutes used to lower returning spacecraft are also automatically released once the spacecraft touches down in the water.

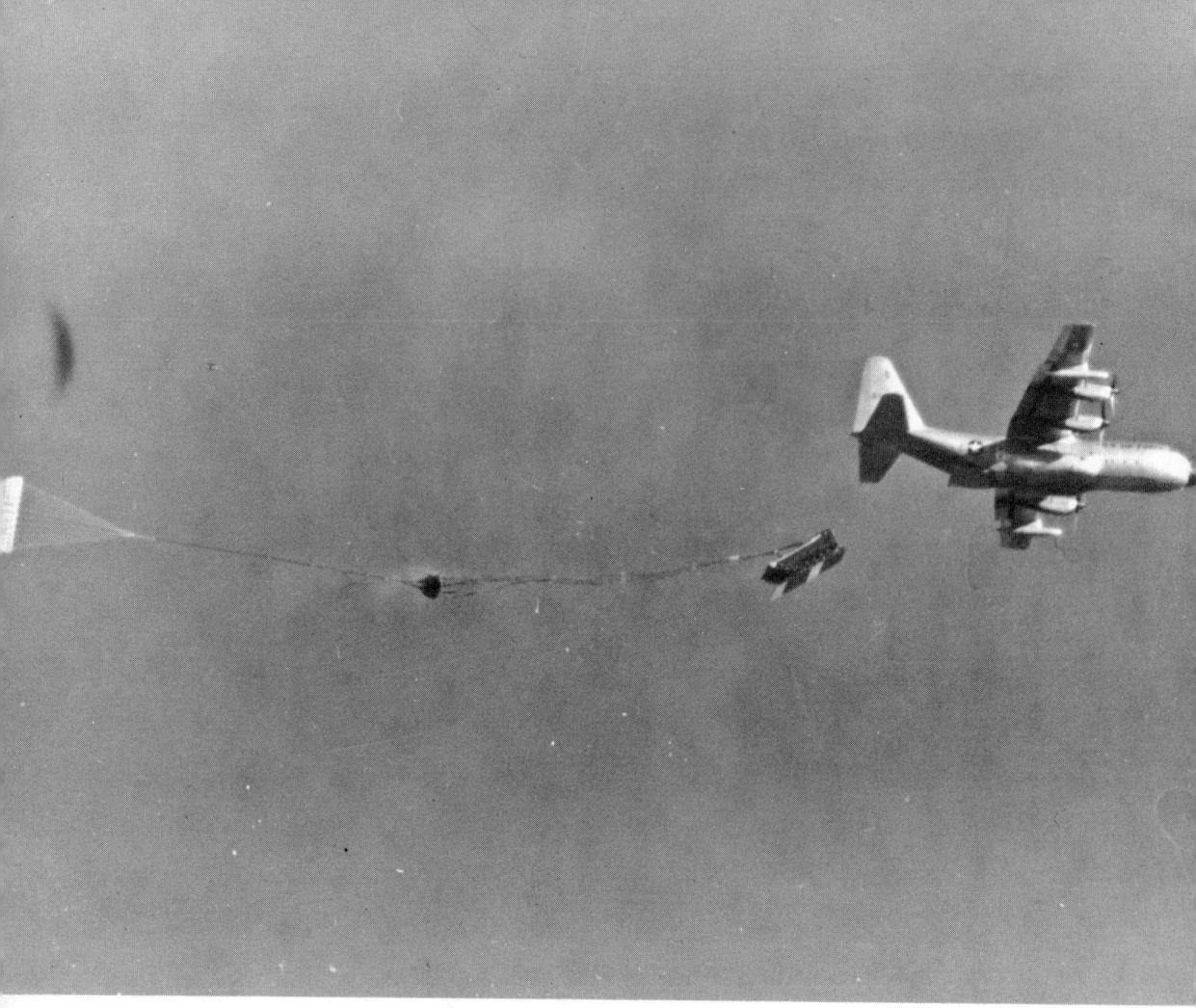

Flying Lance and Jeeps

Thanks to new developments in parachutes and in packing techniques, almost anything can be dropped to ground troops with a good chance it will land in usable condition. In the photo above, for example, a self-propelled tracked launching vehicle for the Lance supersonic surface-to-surface missile is being dropped by chute. The white chute at the left is the drag chute used to eject the vehicle from the cargo plane. This chute also pulls out the six main canopies used to lower the vehicle. On the opposite page (top) is a three-quarter-ton military vehicle being lowered by two huge chutes. Below, a whole "stick" of jeeps drifts down on triple chutes from the cargo aircraft in the distance. Between the jeeps small chutes can be seen lowering packaged supplies, possibly fuel drums. There also seem to be a few objects falling without parachutes. These may be pieces of shock-absorbing material that have torn loose from the jeep platforms or packaged supplies that have torn free from the small parachutes designed to lower them safely.

GPE Saves Time

Not all parachutes are used to drop loads from great heights. In some cases, the canopies are used to unload aircraft without landing, almost at grass level. This technique is known as GPE (ground proximity extraction). It enables aircraft to unload supplies, trucks, weapon systems, and almost anything else except personnel, without landing and taking off again. If the cargo is extracted close enough to the ground, the drop is a matter of only a few feet. The chute not only eases the cargo's fall but slows its forward speed at the same time. Above, a jeep is extracted from a speeding CV-2 Caribou during a demonstration by the 612th Quartermaster Company at Fort Bragg, North Carolina. On the opposite page (top), a pallet loaded with fuel is extracted from a C-130 Hercules. At center, a small truck is shown just after touchdown and in the bottom photo, a similar pallet of supplies is extracted via the GPE system on a frozen lake in Alaska. The GPE system eliminates the need for the aircraft to land, unload supplies, and then take off again, perhaps on dangerous terrain or while under enemy fire.

Pull That Clevis Pin!

Although many cargo air drops are carried out by automatically releasing parachutes that float free once the cargo has touched down, small and medium-sized cargo chutes may not be equipped with automatic releases. In such cases someone has to be right on the spot to pull the pin on the clevis fitting which holds the canopy to the cargo harness. Above, two members of the 557th Quartermaster Company wrestle to free the huge chutes from their cargo load which has just landed. On the opposite page you can get an idea of the size of one of these chutes in comparison with a man. You can readily see how a chute canopy could drag a load of cargo along the ground in a high wind, if it was not either deflated at once or unhitched immediately. The lower photo shows clearly how even a small man-sized cargo chute can drag a 200-pound case of ammunition. Sometimes the "flight" isn't over when the cargo is on the ground! The science of parachuting has come a long way since the first chute was tested, but there are still some problems for ingenious minds to solve.

Floating Firebee

Parachutes are used for a variety of purposes, from saving lives to saving money. For example, huge sums of money are saved by returning the expensive Firebee targets safely to earth to fly again. The Firebee is an ingenious, radio-controlled target drone used for aerial combat practice by pilots of our armed services. These RPV's (remotely piloted vehicles), both subsonic and the newer supersonic Firebees II's, were developed by Teledyne Ryan Aeronautical of San Diego, California, to provide realistic aerial target practice for our sharpshooting combat pilots. Above, a standard Firebee is lowered on its chute after being "shot down." On the opposite page is a newer technique developed to retrieve these expensive "clay pigeons." The technique, known as MARS (midair retrieval system), works as follows: After the mission has been completed (upper left to lower right), the drone ejects a parachute which slows it down. This chute, in turn, pulls out a bigger canopy below it. This canopy opens to lower the target, leaving the smaller chute above it. The smaller chute is 18 feet across; the larger is 79 feet in diameter. A CH-3 helicopter equipped with a special device snares the smaller chute and releases the big canopy, then flies home with the drone and gently lowers it to the ground for servicing and almost immediate reuse, saving both time and money for the marksmen and the taxpayers.

Brake it Gently!

The high landing speed of jet aircraft requires that some military aircraft have more than just brakes on the wheels. As far back as the 1940's, parachutes were used to slow down high-speed aircraft once it was on the ground. Above, at Andrews Air Force Base, Maryland, in February, 1949, a Boeing B-47 Stratojet bomber of the 600-mph class, with a gross weight of about 185,000 pounds, uses a single big brake chute to help it stop. On the opposite page (bottom) one of the earlier models of the North American XB-70 used three drag chutes to slow its 500,000 pounds after landing. These chutes are what are known as ribbon chutes, which used strips of material instead of a solid canopy. The opening between the ribbons permitted air to escape when the first shock of the chute opening occurred; this prevented destruction of the chute. The XB-70, named the Valkyrie, was flown at speeds up to three times that of sound and to more than 70,000 feet to obtain data for the development of the supersonic transport, since abandoned. The bomber version was designed to carry nuclear weapons. Opposite page, top, a most unusual drag chute designed by David T. Barish. This drag or brake chute with sail-like panels revolves when in use. It is known as the vortex ring parachute and is the first major design change in the parachute since it was first invented.

Funny Car Safety Chute

Any object traveling at high speed—aircraft, racing car, or falling paratrooper, needs something to slow it down and stop it. Since the parachute has been proved effective in stopping high-speed aircraft or at least slowing it down enough for wheel brakes to be effective, drivers of specialized racing cars have adopted it for their own uses. Above, a so-called Funny Car is slowed down dramatically at the end of its high-speed run down a drag strip. The brake chute is composed of six panels which form a cross, with double thickness where the panels cross in the center. Such chutes are carried in the back of the vehicle and are released by pulling a knob either on the dashboard or at some other easy-to-reach spot in the cockpit. These chutes can be used at the end of a normal run or if the car threatens to go out of control during the run.

One Plus Two Equals Safe Stop

Here is another example of the use of parachutes to stop a high-speed drag racer at the end of its run. This dragster uses two canopies to help bring the vehicle to a safe stop. The two chutes give double safety; if one should fail, the other would swing to the center and take over the braking assignment in a fraction of a second. This has special value in case of a tire failure, fire, or steering malfunction. These chute canopies are made from tough split-resisting nylon, and they are designed to be flexible enough to take the opening shock repeatedly without damage. Although the speed of these dragsters is high, it is not sufficiently high to require the ribbon-type chutes used to stop high-speed aircraft in landings. These two exceptionally fine photos were taken by Leslie Lovett of the National Hot Rod Association, noted for his outstanding photos of all types of racing cars in action.

U.S. Forest Service Smoke Jumpers

Thanks to the dedicated men and their parachutes, many a forest fire has been beaten before it could become a raging monster. The United States Forest Service, of the Department of Agriculture, uses parachutes in its never-ending battle against forest fires. Highly skilled fire fighters are dropped into the area of the fire to knock it down as soon as possible after it is spotted. They wear special protective clothing and face masks, in case they land in trees, and carry descending ropes to use if they have to get down from a tree-snagged chute in a hurry, radios, and emergency kits for almost any situation. Supplies are also dropped by chute for them to use once they are on the ground. Above, three smoke jumpers in their gear. Note their face masks, high collars, reserve chutes, and heavy gloves. On the opposite page, the top photo shows jumpers on their way down to a fire area. At center, they are shedding their chutes, jump suits, and harnesses to get ready to become fire fighters. The bottom photo shows containers of supplies being dropped close by. These supplies include food, water, axes, saws, flares to start backfires, and many other special items. Parachutes make forest fire fighting quicker and more effective.

Astronauts Learn How to Dunk

Our astronauts receive training for every conceivable emergency, including situations where they may have to bail out over water. Although most of them have worn parachutes previously, not many of them have ever had to make a water parachute landing. They learn how at Lake Texoma, near Sherman, Texas, at a course given by the USAF Air Defense Command Life Support School at Perrin Air Force Base. The astronauts wear open parachutes. They are lifted over the lake, towed by a speedboat, and are then dropped into the water, where they must get out of their chutes, inflate life jackets or a rubber raft, and await rescue. Above, an astronaut seems to walk on water as he begins his flight from the beach out over the lake. The opposite page (top) shows an astronaut about to release from the towboat. He has already partially inflated his lifesaving equipment and let out other equipment on a tether line to keep it within reach when he cuts loose from his chute. The lower photo shows him just as he splashes down. He will release the chute and climb into his small raft. Some astronauts may use their wet flight suits as sails and sail back to the shore. Of course, parachutes are useless in space because there is no air, but an astronaut must be prepared for anything anywhere else.

NASA's Parawings and Paragliders

The parachute, with various modifications, plays an important part in NASA's many programs. The National Aeronautics and Space Administration has developed some startling versions of Leonardo da Vinci's simple pyramidal parachute. Above, left, is a parawing, or gliding parachute, as big as a B-47. It has a wing span of 110 feet, an area of 4,000 square feet of coated nylon, and is capable of gliding flight with a load of up to 3 tons. This experimental model indicates that a full-scale model should be able to land carrying a load of as much as 18,000 pounds. The center photo shows another NASA experimental parawing lowering a model of a lifting-body spacecraft, and the photo at upper right shows a NASA paraglider with air-filled tubular struts in experimental flight with a dummy space vehicle as a cargo. On the opposite page is a NASA paraglider with a length of 20 feet, gliding down under radio control after being released from a helicopter at 4,000 feet. It is carrying a 6-foot-long model of a lifting-body reentry vehicle as its cargo. NASA, concerned with everything that has to do with space and aeronautics, is finding new ways to use the parachute.

Rehearsal and "For Real"

Before entrusting returning astronauts to a parachute landing, NASA scientists conducted many experiments with what is called a boilerplate test vehicle. This exact replica in size and weight of a returning spacecraft was test dropped from an aircraft at 13,000 feet using a cluster of three 88-foot ringsail parachutes. The replica of the Apollo command module floated down (above) at a speed of 25 feet per second to a safe water landing. The success of the tests has been demonstrated many times now by the safe landing of all our returning command modules with their precious human crews. On the opposite page is the "for real" landing of the Apollo 15 command module. It landed safely although one of the three chutes collapsed. The top photo shows the startling landing with only two chutes; below, the safe landing a moment after splashdown. Air is spilling from the chutes just before they are automatically released to drift away. The chute that failed to inflate properly is in the center.

Welcome Sight to Millions!

A welcome sight to millions of people is a returning command module swinging gently under three brilliantly colored ringsail parachutes after a successful trip to the moon and back. This seems a fitting last picture for the book. May all space flights end as happily as did this landing of Apollo 14, thanks to space-age chutes.